516 y

Shapes

David Kirkby

Heinemann

First published in Great Britain by Heinemann Library
an imprint of Heinemann Publishers (Oxford) Ltd
Halley Court, Jordan Hill, Oxford OX2 8EJ

MADRID ATHENS PARIS
FLORENCE PRAGUE WARSAW
PORTSMOUTH NH CHICAGO SAO PAULO
SINGAPORE TOKYO MELBOURNE AUCKLAND
IBADAN GABERONE JOHANNESBURG

Designed by The Pinpoint Design Company
Printed in China

99 98 97 96 95
10 9 8 7 6 5 4 3 2 1

ISBN 0431 07959 5

British Library Cataloguing in Publication Data available on
request from the British Library.

Acknowledgements
The Publishers would like to thank the following
for the kind loan of equipment and materials
used in this book: Boswells, Oxford; The Early Learning
Centre; Lewis', Oxford; W. H. Smith; N. E. S. Arnold; Tumi.
Special thanks to the children of St Francis C.E. First School

The Publishers would like to thank the following for
permission to reproduce photographs: J. Allan Cash Ltd. p 10;
Robert Harding Picture Library p 20.
All other photographs: Chris Honeywell, Oxford

Cover photograph: Chris Honeywell, Oxford

Contents

A square has 4 straight sides, all the same length. It has 4 matching corners.

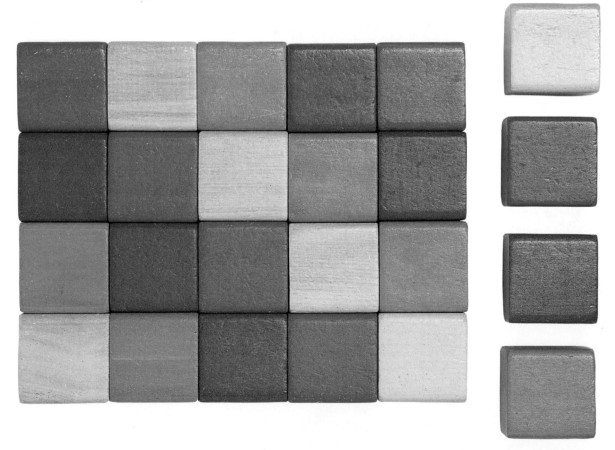

Squares tessellate.
They fit together with no gaps.

How many squares can you see?

To do:
Draw a house with
4 square windows.
Draw a big square.
Make 4 squares
tessellate inside it.

A rectangle has
4 straight sides.
It often has
2 long sides and
2 short sides.
It has 4 matching
corners.

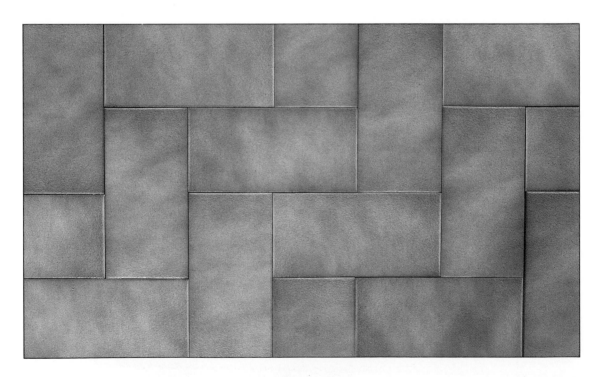

Rectangles tessellate.
They fit together with no gaps.

How many rectangles can you see?

To do:
Draw a rug.
Make a tessellating
pattern on it
with rectangles.

A triangle has 3 straight sides. The corners do not need to match.

This triangle has sides of the same length. Some triangles have sides of different lengths.

How many triangles can you see?

To do:
Draw the fattest
triangle you can.
Draw the thinnest
triangle you can.

These are circles.
A circle has no
corners.

This target has
circles inside circles.

How many circles can you see?

To do:
Draw some circles.
Do circles tessellate?

A cube is a solid shape.
It is not flat.
It has 6 faces
(sides).
Each face is a
square.

Some food is cube shaped.

How many pictures can the cube puzzle make?

To do:
Copy this shape.
Cut it out and make
a cube.

13

A cuboid is a solid shape.
It has 6 faces (sides).
These faces can be rectangles or squares.

These cuboids are all the same size.

How many cuboids can you see?

To do:
Find a cuboid.
How many faces
does it have?
Are the faces all the
same size?

A cylinder is a solid shape.

It is tube shaped.

The end faces are circles.

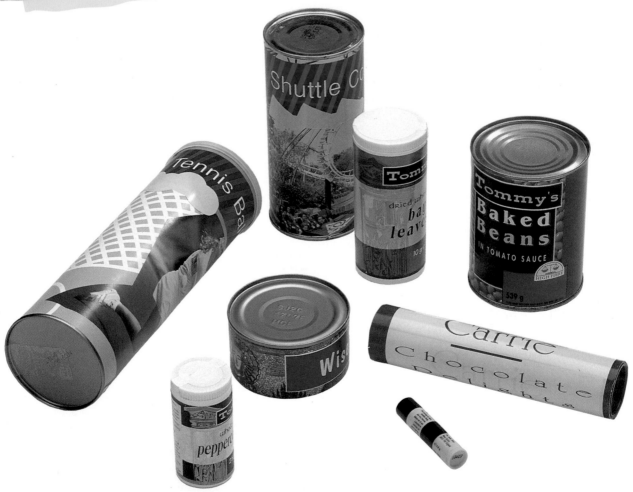

These are all cylinders.

How many cylinders can you see?

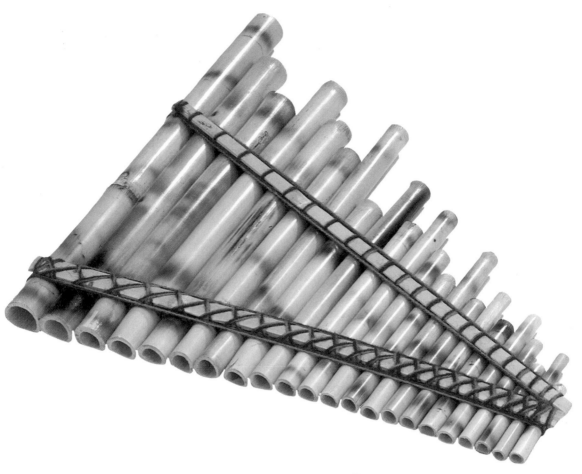

To do:
Can you make a tower using cylinders on their ends?
What happens when you try to make a tower using cylinders on their sides?

A sphere is a solid shape.
It is round.
A ball is a sphere.

A sphere is good to roll.

18

How many spheres
can you see?

To do:
Can you make a tower
from cubes?
Can you make a tower
from cuboids?
Can you make a tower
from spheres?

A pyramid is a solid shape.

It has triangle shaped sides that join at the top.

It can have a different shape for a base (bottom).

Pyramids can be very big.

How many of these pyramids have square shaped bases?

To do:
How many sides does a pyramid with a square base have?
How many sides does a pyramid with a triangle shaped base have?

A cone is a solid
shape.
It has a circle for
a base.

These are all cones.

The tops of these are cone shaped.
How many cones can you see?

To do:
Copy this shape onto
paper or card.
Cut it out.
Make a cone shape.

GLUE

answers

---

index